THE TRIUMPH OF CANCER

Chris McCabe's work crosses artforms and genres including fiction, non-fiction, drama and visual art. His poetry has been recorded for the Poetry Archive and he was shortlisted for the Ted Hughes Award in 2013. He has published four collections of poetry, including the highly praised *Speculatrix* (2014), and his work has been described by *The Guardian* as 'an impressively inventive survey of English in the 21st century'. His psychogeographic books about London's cemeteries, *In the Catacombs* and *Cenotaph South*, are published by Penned in the Margins. With Victoria Bean he is the co-editor of *The New Concrete: Visual Poetry in the 21st Century* (Hayward Publishing, 2015) and his first novel, *Dedalus*, a sequel to *Ulysses*, was published by Henningham Family Press in 2018. He works as the Librarian at the National Poetry Library, Southbank Centre.

ALSO BY CHRIS MCCABE

POETRY

The Hutton Inquiry (Salt Publishing, 2005)
Zeppelins (Salt Publishing, 2008)
THE RESTRUCTURE (Salt Publishing, 2012)
Speculatrix (Penned in the Margins, 2014)

AS EDITOR

The New Concrete: Visual Poetry in the 21st Century
    (with Victoria Bean; Hayward Publishing, 2015)

NON-FICTION

In the Catacombs (Penned in the Margins, 2014)
Cenotaph South (Penned in the Margins, 2016)
Real South Bank (Seren, 2016)

VERSE DRAMA

Shad Thames, Broken Wharf (Penned in the Margins, 2010)

FICTION

Dedalus (Henningham Family Press, 2018)

The Triumph of Cancer

Chris McCabe

Penned in the Margins
LONDON

PUBLISHED BY PENNED IN THE MARGINS
Toynbee Studios, 28 Commercial Street, London E1 6AB
www.pennedinthemargins.co.uk

First published 2018

Printed in the United Kingdom by TJ International

ISBN
978-1-908058-60-7

CONTENTS

Crab	15
X-ray	16
Cell	17
Balloon	18
Mrs Merton	19
Snooker	20
Cancer	21
Clatterbridge	25
Heimlich	26
Snowglobe	27
Cinema	28
Pinthover	29
Metastasis	30
Alice	31
Love	34
Chipfork	35
Kipper	37

Hedgehog 39

Starling 41

Lungworm 42

Pornography 43

Worm 44

Easter 45

Oncologist 47

Hodgkin's 48

Slug 49

Wound 50

Brick 51

Face 52

& 54

Light 56

Voice 57

Campfire 58

U-bend 59

Sea 60

Lemon 62

Owl Pellet   63

Rabbit   64

Car   65

Vertigo   67

Library   70

Cure   73

August   74

Anarchitecture   75

Straw   76

Body   78

Cemetery   79

No Word   81

Bowie   82

Pink   83

Stockings   85

Coupling   86

Anchor   87

Ditch   88

ACKNOWLEDGEMENTS   89

For Sarah and Pavel, in everything

'This body of ours, this disguise put on by common jumping molecules, is in constant revolt against the abominable farce of having to endure. Our molecules, the dears, want to get lost in the universe as fast as they can!'

LOUIS-FERDINAND CELINE, *Journey to the End of the Night*
(transl. JOHN BANVILLE)

'For out of much more, out of little not much, out of nothing nothing: in these sprays at all events there is a new world of inscape.'

GERARD MANLEY HOPKINS, Journal, 1871

The
Triumph
of
Cancer

Crab

In a tropic of crabs what bad shorts
and high socks did you wear as you wiped blood
from your finger, cut by the claw
of forearm guns that clutched back at the tides
of the only sea that could sway them?
That crab the Greeks used to give cancer its name,
how it spreads sideways out, like fingers, outwards;
karkinos, Hippocrates called it,
that could only be treated with a cauterized tool
called the Fire Drill. The summer's elastic starched;
you laughed, saying you're fine, it's a nick,
as we watched the reddened fleck break & asked
can we keep it dad, we asked & asked
as you put the crab back,
the crab you always put back.

X-ray

Pierre & Marie Curie met in 1894 through their fascination with magnetism. They married a year later. *Radium, be near to me.* Where so many patients have seen their death through radioactivity they saw each other. Like the writer that chokes on their pen, the breakthrough fluid Marie held in her hands killed her [leukemia]. Their daughter, Irene, disappeared into the future.

One evening, decades before, Pierre had walked through rain along the Rue Dauphine & slipped under a horse-drawn cart, crushing his skull unto death. *Radium, be near to me.* His father & lab assistant both said the same thing : his mind was elsewhere, thinking of a cure for cancer.

Cell

it, it, it, it, it, it, it

it, it, it, it, it, it, it

it, it, it, it, it, it, it

it, it, it, @ it, it, it

it, it, it, it, it, it, it

it, it, it, it, it, it, it

it, it, it, it, it, it, it

Balloon

Balloons are stillborn cysts
resistant to sustenance;
they sucker-up to the teat & start to swell,
suckling limp with a flaccid feebleness.
They flare with growth, all-belly,
stretch their magenta to a viscous puce,
sucking-up each drop in a taughtening façade
until their death poises pertinent to a touch.
They halt, withdraw : a plastic vellum
on which the world is writ.
The runt hisses a filthy Latin,
puckers its mouth into a wrinkled O
tight as a carp's & stares :
its starved eye intent only on eating.

It flies to the pen of its siblings.

Mrs Merton

i.m. Caroline Aherne, 1963-2016

born with cancer of the eyes
as if to watch
what grows in silence
as if to see to what waits to disperse
at the centre of perception
in the luminous world
where the outline of the sun
is the same black ring
as the after-image
of the liquid rings
that cast a shadow back
to the globe of Saturn

Snooker

i.m Paul Hunter

'cancer, we now know, is a disease cause by the
uncontrolled growth of a single cell'
                    SIDDHARTHA MUKHERJEE

the tight static under the light
and the stellae of dust around
the baize as the balls are placed
in the triangle & the player stands
back astonished to see the red
mutate into reds & the white
swallowed in reds endless reds
the baize lost to primary ivories
no space for hand for cue for control
the balls fly out across slate bed
the player leans forward into chaos
leans forward moves no more a cloth
is pulled across. this could run all night.

Cancer

'That was a way of putting it, not very satisfactory'
T.S. ELIOT

It's difficult, underground, to ask the question forgotten.
The feeling of unresolved emotion nags : herald moths
blown from the loculi. There is a structure, a crosshatch of DNA,
that becomes sentience, discernible in a flickering hindwing,
an eyebrow raised past words that ceased. Susurrations
of dissatisfaction in the shutters of the Tube, at Queen's Park
or Kings X, the networks out on phones still touched,
held to chests while motion moves motion towards connections :
the signal of completion. *No, she said, not that : I don't want it.*
And the Tube started. To say she alighted would simplify how
          heavy
it feels to move forward alone, away from the dance of endorphins
which takes place twice, three times in a person's life : the real
so often ruse of new beginnings. Traces of dust in the laughter
          lines.
I take cash from the ATM, switch to the DLR & check my texts.
One in eight men will get cancer of the prostate. The news is out.

It occurs to me that people have two existing problems :
the inevitable & hope. The sea belches gas & we call it freshness.
So this is the limit then. Foundations become facts.
If Ian Curtis had not killed himself he'd have had a solo career.
The blind man's dog has no concept of leisure. Late at night
after three carafes we walked to Blackfriars Bridge & ran our hands
over the scars of the Blitz. The same questions of money :
the bank manager in awe of the poet whispers in his ear :
you perhaps will need to look for work again? This is the new way
asked by Rainer Werner Fassbinder. The poet has eyes of water.
Life, at first, is about using our energy well : then we learn to lose it
without gravitas. Stopcocks replaced with LCDs.
A reconstructed lectern in a Wetherspoons is a ranter's paradise.
The Oktoberfest lasts for years. In moments of social awkwardness
zips give us something to think with. If you'd have asked me direct,
back then, things would have been different. In my commute begins
the death of my prime. Cells beneath my eyes ceased to renew
at millennium's birth : if they rejuvenate at my peak they eat the
    flesh.
Cancer, as such, is burnout : those who dance in their nineties
are just fading away. Now childhood is full of absences.
Coffee's worse for the heart I heard. Bob Monkhouse lost his
    jokebook,

then his prostate burned its starform. At least he knew his jokes.
Bob had a last one for the road. One for the hill. Then disappeared
into the valley of archived Betamax. He glowed in orange (in grief
for his dead son) while his own flesh ate his marrow.
He gave his last live night with red cells balloting the white.
The complexity of humans is enmeshed in their cancer risk : Peto's
Paradox : large multi-celled organisms should show further
propensity for the disease, but don't. We churn ourselves through
misuse but Mark E. Smith is already sixty. My heart is somewhere
	else
in the plastic of oceans & the part-cremation of my habits.
Life's O bituary then you die, with all good cells crying out to
	the end :
I'm Spartacus!
I have learnt to inject solids. Life dates facts like soiled inkjets.
Cancer cells are greedheads, nocturnal movers of neighbours'
	fences.
Your Albion splits into opposing Zoas. Los at the furnace beats
an anvil. Our body's a cuckoo egg hollowed of yolk, submerged
in vinegar. The mind says : I will fight this to the last of my
	enzymes
but what is it, *exactly*, that I'm fighting? The doctor blinks.
If he was a theorist, he would answer : cancer is rhizomatic, the

root stalk

like the surface of a body of water, spreads towards all available
space, eroding what's in its way. Your cancer craves equilibrium,
to be all the spaces it is not. The Tube pulls in at Mile End.
The banker too gets cancer : with follicle knots he turns to dust.
The Tube has stalled, the light flutters. Hold me. Hold my hand
    now.
Don't text. I was told until the age of twelve that every cancer
    victim
had died of old age. In reality they were young & their cells in
    growth.
Au revoir all Peter Pans! Now your cells fly the stratosphere.
Someone forgot to pause the baby. We must think of cells, in the
    end,
as the novice on the ice rink, life as the lines left in the surface,
after the dance. This is cancer's triumph.

Clatterbridge

There was a man my dad drove for treatment
who'd lost his penis.
I didn't know you could get it there, I said.
My dad said : you can get it anywhere.
Clatterbridge : even the hospital sounded
like lives falling apart.
Minutes passed & Peugeot's eternity arrived at school gates.
I said, listen : you don't need it after a certain age anyway.
He said : need what?
I said : your penis.
He said : I'd like it just in case.

Heimlich

Sinusitis is a kind of plague, the Boy says,
and there is no treatment for cancer.
We're travelling by Pendolino,
slick pendulum; it tilts at the bends.
The newspaper tell us that Heimlich
used his manoeuvre this week over dinner,
forty years after his invention,
and felt theory pork itself into practice
straight from the survivor's oesophagus.

Snowglobe

And what are you looking at now, the journalist asks. *Can you see the dead there? Have they been removed?* My son is sad at the top of the stairs because he's smashed his snowglobe. Green glitter in the red carpet's weave. The witness says, *It's quite difficult to talk right now, if I'm honest, I'm still in shock.* I tell my son we can buy another, that you don't lose luck from broken glass. And I'm still refusing the wine. *Luckily I was at the back of the bar with my wife*, the man says. A splinter of glass is in my toe. The snowglobe was a gift bought passing through Dublin airport last month. It had a little town in it.

Cinema

Cancer changed him more than my arsenic asides or the matinées he drove me to on Saturday afternoons. It took his speech, for one thing. But then, when did I ever let him speak? Driving the concretised beachways of the north's A-roads I'd throw things in to make sure he was still listening. Light of my life, from the fire of his loins I arrived to ask. To ask if he'd drive me to the edge of the world cinema on a Saturday to watch *A Clockwork Orange*? Saturdays were chores & compensatory rest but he surprised us both by saying *Yes*. I locked him into a long joke in the popcorn queue. Did I want him to watch the film or just for him to watch me watch it? The film got in the way : the uncut version that seemed to run for hours. *What exactly is the treatment here going to be then? Quite simple really : we're just going to show you some film.* Violence set to Beethoven meant nothing to us. Afterwards the car's interior was dumbed by May heat. *What did you think?* I asked. *It was okay, a bit long.* Lo-lee-ta. Anecdotes on Joyce & Sterne. Stein at breakfast. Unasked for Hopkins. Cancer, in the end, was more avant-garde.

Pinthover

after G.M. Hopkins' 'The Windhover'

An unaccepted pint is a cubed kestrel, hovering on the wind.
Dauphin of the dulled moment's resistance, this evening's
evening crown stood chilled there above an oak beam,
then off to down with a swig, the gut & glug chicaning the pining
gullet as it smooths the throat's glovepurse, the glow in the mind
of this glyph refused, the regalia of it, the crystal tardis of the thing!
Amber & wheat clouds to thrushes as it stirs the mind
from familiar grooves & the fire breaks in unexpected converse,
incomparable to the archived inbox & committee's wet tinder.
No wonder of this : sabbatical fabric rips like face cloths
and the mind shines, O my director, emphatic Erdinger,
take wing your banknote to browngold sustenance!

Metastasis

The spleen spits out
cells like a Penny Falls,
rapacious as locusts
to be where it lacks.
The stuck switch
clones its duff.
New currencies
windfall the trough.

Alice

'She set to work, and very soon finished off the cake.

```
*    *    *    *
  *    *    *
*    *    *    *'
```

LEWIS CARROLL, *Alice in Wonderland*

ARGUMENT

If Alice's body was not a telescope it would stay outside a
    catflap.
If it was not shrinkable it could not ask 'Who am I then?'
If it was not able to grow it would change by night.
When a sign says EAT ME she eats. DRINK ME tastes of
    cherry.
Her body of text disappears in asterisks. Asterisks to the
    ancient Greeks
meant *little stars*. Wikipedia says Alice's asterisks are section
    breaks.
Asterisks in *Alice* are Alice's ellipses of thought. Her body
    goes out like little stars.

She reappears through alterations. The telescope is back-to-front.

Asterisks can be used in censorship & consumption can be censorship.

Late Latin : *asteriscus*. We are getting asteriscus. Six-pronged flakes

that cover vowels. Consonants are more commonly concealed by asterisks.

The name Alice is only forty percent consonants. Alice then is mostly vowels.

A girl in the text could be an upside-down question mark,

only — she is not — she is asterisks. Muddled & inquisitive & lost.

Thirty-six asterisks to be exact. Mathematicians also call these *stars*.

Black snow on yellow. And Alice turns to stars whenever she eats.

*   *   *   *
    *   *   *
*   *   *   *

POEM

Alice's body turns to stars
after DRINK ME, after the taste of turkey & toffee, she
turns to stars
then is just ten inches high, enough to pass through a
garden gate,
the height of a candle — thinking flame — & she wonders
how it feels to be a candle blown out,
though she's never blown out in text, she's turned to stars,
after she's eaten, in the mystery of consumption,
the miles of intestines stranger than the paths she follows,
she's turned to stars after EAT ME, marked in currants,
but starfields should follow cinnamon,
snowflakes after currants, it is wonderful to have a body
that disappears after excitements & questions & instructions,
to have a body that is turned to stars thirty-six times in one
day,
that is EAT ME that is DRINK ME that is a telescope out
the right way
pointing back to the snowflake of self that melts under its lens.
That melts like black stars becoming the body of Alice.

Love

'love is a thing below a man'
LAURENCE STERNE

Love is a thing below a man,
beneath him, beyond,
a thing too low to stoop for,
a thing in the gutter;
love is a thing for lowlives & thieves,
a thing that thrives where no sun is,
for the selfish & sunblind;
love is a thing where the fall begins.

Let the man fall

Chipfork

Chipforks are like little fish,
little wooden pike flecked in the egg,
mouths agape in inverted Vs,
their seven hundred teeth yet to grow,
each an inch long, but grinning,
like Ted Hughes wrote,
grinning to be made of wood;
they have the knowledge that they'll grow
to eat other pike, ram them down their gullets,
like Ted Hughes said : & even though
their dorsals & rectals are absent,
in the smooth manufacture of their cut,
they'll flourish as olive kings in an algae kingdom,
to be known in a poem read
in every educational institution.
On occasion the splint of thought
bites back at them, that it isn't true,
that their lives are as white plastic knives
to be plucked from a box at midnight

and given to the drunk
on greaseproofed slates,
to be gently raised to amber lights
like brittle keys for forgotten locks.

Kipper

Kippers must have burst their livers;
jaundiced lenses
swim a sallow dish.
Split back flatfish of kippers.
Mirror of recto
verso in reflectors :
both sides real for kippers.
In Kerouac's last hours in New Mexico
eyes flushed sepias
slowly ambered like kippers.
Kippers' livers shoot
cod oil from hot spoons
to give them eyes of dying drinkers.
Boys age; one man in every twelve
takes drink as substance,
twelve in every 100,000
washed up on the shore,
shivering post-*Chivas Regal*,
bruisemarks on their arms striped like kippers.

For they fight against the tide
when faced with death's turbulence;
the head that tugs the nervous system
thrashes for life : both men & kippers.
In Andorra I drank twelve double vodkas
mixed with *Crazy Horses*
in a bar run by Scousers,
nerves like pan-fried langoustines;
at such altitude
asthma & palpitations
took me to the top apartment
besides Fat Eddie's bunk —
I thought he'd know what to say.
Fat Eddie said, Ride it out, get some kip,
and I did for two days until I had to eat
and the first thing that looked back at my face
after the mirror's hotplate
was the upside-down shoal of the dawn-fish,
a scent that sings
that aubade of health I'd heard before :
the fretless violins of kippers.

Hedgehog

All human death is in the hedgehog,
under its wig I mean, the way we think.
The one that drowned itself three times
until we took it from the bank,
nursed in a cycle helmet,
its whole body a mortified punk,
corpse in plexus panic, slipping with each breath
like Roy Orbison's toupée in the video to 'Crying'.
As we crossed the bridge its claws gripped
like the hands of a hundred-year-old man
charred in an air raid bunker,
its face a rubber dog,
rasping at the grille of a respirator.
We took it deep into woodland
and he saw us, his face of the sixties' bassist,
back flecked starlike as a starling,
pushed down into earth,
all snout & breath, until he stilled
his back of a thousand quills —

each firing skywards in a parody
of the poet's brain — contrite as Rimbaud,
dead on his feet, limping to Africa.

Starling

Like a glam bass player ousted
by the kingfisher's cover shot,
face pinched to a barber-surgeon's mask,
neurotic on their own
but in the pack the Mods
could not cohere as well as this
to flickblades & engines
along Brighton's coast.
The crow, hooded king, craws
like a Rocker's bike & the crowd scatters
the tide's break —
one starling stands, lifting its legs
like stilts sucked back from sand.
Hysterical as a jester at the queen's wake.

Lungworm

'The word has gone viral'
WILLIAM BURROUGHS

Lesions licked from silvered slug trails,
the stipplestick of death.
You drink the host from a viral chalice
in whispers softer than sparrows' air tracts.

Words burrow through earthsoil,
pass the long wait of bitterwort & the white
palette of expectation : your face.

All the worms, each double-ended word,
the poison from the skin before the de-crowning leveller bit in.
You were our King's taster. When you died you grew
from the other end & the sparrow ate your head.

Silence came too late.
This virus is in us.

Pornography

'the gentle pornography found in hedgerows'
TOM JENKS

Albion's hedges were littered with pornography. Bushes fluffed with shreds of *Frazzle*. The hawthorn's back was up, like a pigeon's ruff. Gutters dealt out playing cards : legs parted in far-off limousines. Shoes trundled from cut-off wire. Space hoppers shrivelled like scrotums at sea.

The internet does it cleaner & everything moves. It was easier to hide a rummy hand beneath your shorts than close down three windows. Behind each one a leprechaun winks above a golden pot. What does roulette have to do with it?

Albion's streets are relieved. Sparrows are on the incline. Cigarette packs carry warnings for the grown-ups. It's hard not to look. Throats exposed to holes & growths.

Flesh never used to look like this.

Worm

'The invisible worm
... flies in the night'
WILLIAM BLAKE 'The Sick Rose'

Invisible worm you are immortal
    a banded muscle
cut by boys into tapas rings
    barbed by a hook
in the howling stream
    slipped back to earth
beyond the carp's gold eye
    divided & multiplied
    divided & multiplied
    divided & multiplied
in the night, beneath the gale
you fattened like a leather band
    sealed a caul around metallic sinews
    sourced a blood supply
    like a nightcharmed cobra
and while the creature who cut you fifty years before slept —
    you grew

Easter

Today is Easter & the stars have slept through.
A dressing gown might pass as an attempt
to be Christ-like but Shiva would be a better mentor.
When every cell in our bodies
was formed not on earth but in the depths
of space, what were you ever doing here? —
painting a kitchen wall, waiting for a kettle to boil.
The life cycle of the stars shows what is in us;
as rapid as cancer cells, they burst a nebula,
a stella nursery, explode in life.
There's rain on the window that vacant glass
can't cancel. Those stars that burned for years
blow up for want of food, become giants
bigger than the sun – devour their tails
like pink sharks in the uterus. Every atom
in your body started life as something else,
so what is there to complain about?
Medicine is the negative reprint after the party.
You are made of the same basic ingredients

as a dinosaur or a rock — definitely a rock. Sip,

look at the plants — chemicals connect us. This

is the earth's endless variety, from gold to post-it.

Proxima centauri is burning in your anatomy.

Sodium simmers yellow, potassium lilac, copper blue.

What do you think of cremation?

Stars die for want of hydrogen, swell, darken :

in their core exists a futile battle with gravity.

Each element has its own characteristic colour

which tells us what the stars are made of.

A billion billion billion carbon atoms in one person.

We come from stars; for us to live stars must die.

Do we really need to look up to know complex matter?

Outside, foil eggs are hidden in the plant pots & grass.

Someone put them there.

Oncologist

'Didacus Valzquius, Pictor Regis, Expinxit'

Diego Velázquez, Painter to the King, Unpainted this
DIEGO VELAZQUEZ

As king's painter
only he can erase;
disappearance
too has kinship
to the creation
of doors, windows,
popes, dwarves —
the king can command
that the horse must go,
but only Velázquez
can unpaint this.

Hodgkin's

Some cancers are magicians. Some are shy, concealers of threat, some terrorists. They disperse like salmon up spinal fluid, stake out the brain.

Hodgkin's is an architect : builder of lymph nodes in semi-solid, gritted liquid; not of flesh, outside of blood, cells blunder up like desk magnets. Skywards to clavicle, a city forms. The bump on the neck is the tip of the high-rise.

With Hodgkin's you know who you were.

Slug

Years are measured in slugs.
How you rolled yourself in sweat
through the gyre of linen
all the nightwaved summer long.
Drank, ate, slept an hour :
woke. The tan kept the toxins
from your face. Slowly, then slowly,
the clock stopped its throat
as the slugs masticated the salt
of each second : they could not
be stopped. Like men burned
in polyester sleeping bags,
darkness is their water,
their blood saliva, a shorthand
written in daggers & stars.
You descend to the charred desert
of coffee & ash. 6:58.
One hundred slugs have passed.
The tracks are all over your face.

Wound

How could I not love his cancer by then;
it was the last kiss he knew,
the hospice stilled, beyond grievance,
a love that lives in its opposite,
the way the Victorian widow's impulse
was to visit the cell of her husband's murderer
and in mutual gloaming the barred light distils
the fact that brought them to this.
We do not know why but still we dig.
Rossetti unearthed his wife's grave
to take back the poems he'd buried her with,
her hair growing in copper tresses,
the page illegible as the slowworm's bullets,
recalled as if to see the secret wound
that killed her, to know by seeing his words,
as I know for writing, *I loved his cancer.*

Brick

If you had a brick
would you build a house
like the first you knew,
or add it to a wall,
or plant an outhouse
at the end of the path
for all your documents,
using the last brick
to siphon the light
from the windows?

If you had a tumour
would you grind the brick
with a pumice
down to an elixir,
to counter the cells
stacking their seats
into the auditorium
of your death certificate?
Or would you show it the brick
and smash it to fucking bits?

Face

His face which was lit
Which was
Which, lit his face
Like a book
Could be read like a
A facebook which was
Was which
Like a switch
His face, lit
Which was
The way it was
Which was the one
Face, the only face which was lit
Like a switch
On a book
On a switch in
A facebook
A face which was like
A face

And was a face
Which could be read
And was enough
Because it
Was the only face he had

&

'Wherein could this flea guilty be,
Except in that drop which it sucked from thee?'
JOHN DONNE

Mark but this &, and mark in full script,
Saw something of ourselves in it before it bit;
Sucked on Blake's amniotic blood
Until the caul was a cut worm's hood,
Nipped dual-pronged into the white,
Drunk then fled into fetish night.
    Icon of symbol & pressèd text,
    Compressed in tied knot of syntax :
    Brought your eye to see in the compact.

Three lines in one & two letters spare,
Like a bald babe curled up bare,
This & is you & this & is I, locked like a 69
On a marriage bed — twinned fizz-pins of wine —
This maverick love our parents grudged
That cloistered in a motorway Travelodge.

Our & a medieval torture trick
For knuckles buckled in its black
Our fingers linked in the gold of wedlock.

Then you said why not just use the 'and'
And while you're there make all rhymes end
Evenly around where the & would be
And file down the serif of the sign for me?
Yet we agree that being together
Is stronger than any visual character :
    But in that first poem the nit of the &
    Bit your eye like light from sand
    In one looped stroke that flew my hand.

Light

i.m. Jackson Mac Low

On the seventh day he split a deck of cards & boiled them
    in stock.
On day three he was named a God of concrete though his
    only light was thought.
On the tenth day he named all the lights the language
    contains.
On day eight he tried to rest but woke in Atomic light.
On the sixth he watched photons split from particle to wave.
The fourth day was spent at Cobbing's tabernacle, Better
    Books.
On the second day he walked the desert's ludic velcro &
    saw a different self in each grain.
On the ninth day he divided his staples between Fluxus &
    poetics.
On the fifth he split the waves & walked the matrix like a
    ghost.

On the first day he made the alphabet.

Voice

for Roddy Lumsden

I'm thinking of a lexical meaning.
You would know what it is.
Or is it a semantic meaning?
You would know what I mean.
It is of the earth & ribbed like tweed,
wild & knitted as a plaque,
when you asked what I meant by that,
after midnight in Holborn,
I said it was a texture I'd heard before,
that you heard in some texts
by poets who are outside of it
and out there by choice.
A texture that starts in the larynx,
flies the earth, catches on plaque.

The word for it was voice. Voice.

Campfire

Stories won't fuel me.
Feed me blank pages
and I'll score them like Hendrix.
Have you seen my chickens?
My chickens are in the forgeworks
popping their claws like corn.
My arthritis is my cremation
and there's nothing poetic about an ember.
Have you seen my chook-chooks?
My taps dance the dusk's hobs
and now your mind can't turn them off.
I lick my own face like a crone in the reeds,
I've been eating with no teeth for centuries.
Have you seen my cockerel?
My prototype drips like tallow from its beak
and my cremation is arthritic.
Have you seen my rooks?
When I sleep they wear their Sunday suits
and say their prayers with the jackdaws.
Blow my embers : here are my crows.

U-bend

for Sarah

I'm down on my knees again,
except I never was before,
not even when the fox asked, Will You?
It's dark down here, at the U-bend,
where your wedding ring flints ruby
in a welter of sugared hair.
Love, it wasn't what we said it was,
when all was red & the sea our end.
I'd do it again. Will you?
Give me the tools & your hand.

Sea

'None grow rich in the sea'
TED HUGHES

No one ever went to sea & regained their youth.

§

A poet who tries to give voice to the sea
finds their black lungs coughed like polyps
into the loquacious spume of the ocean's mouth.

§

Despite its shingling sibilants the sea will only pay cash
to its suicides.

§

The fiddler crab is a seaside bodybuilder
who clutches a dumbbell in just one fist.
Blushing, he crawls to the wings of the Punchset,
clattering his hat to the tide's applause.

§

Only the body spat from the sea is ready for burial.
Breakers bruise grief into the white rind of flesh.
A family gathers on the shore in cinematic stock.
Nephews raise hoods like Druids & watch decades
of agitated sleep simmer to peace in the rockpool's pot.
Police cameras catch redeye like common sunstars.
The suicide zips inside a body bag, tight as a razor clam's flute.

§

Miles of sea peels back to the stamp of the burial plot.
His face pauses in death like a man about to sneeze.

§

He made it inland across snags, hooks, holdfasts & rocks.

§

None grow rich.

Lemon

for Sophie Herxheimer

Lemons are compasses encased with a bacon rind.
Eleven petalled sunflowers sealed like a cheese
and cloned in a bushel. They pluck from the branch
with a catapulted thwack : wax seals the fist.

Owl Pellet

A cremation in a body bag,
skulls, teeth, feathers, claws :
an Index Expurgatorius
coughed from the Pontiff's oesophagus.
The Pontiff stares under his fluffed zucchetto,
hook nosed & cavity-mouthed
and shrieks the compacted bone-turd
from his stomach's chicane.
The prayer is material, a post-mortem *in excelcis Deo*.
If Hieronymus Bosch had worked sculpture
this would be it : inside the faecal matter,
disrobing in water, bones move, claws loosen,
a skull floats in its song-with-no-structure,
rises from the weave of feather
and indigestibles, relieved to feature
in this afterlife : these doubter's notes,
the prayerscript of an observer.

Rabbit

You'll end up with a fat bunny
or a rabbit with diarrhoea
and a messy anus
in which flies will lay eggs
and maggots hatch
to slowly eat bunny
from the inside-out

Car

Poets drive their car to an all night drive-in, alone, lay down
a blanket & masturbate.

The poet's car has three gears : hysterical, delirious & stuck.

Fuel, for the poet, is tanked old tears.

Under the poet's dashboard is an archive of chewing gum,
each one given the colour of a lipstick.

Every poet has a photograph of the car they wrote their first
poem in. Here, look.

In the backseat, poets watch pornography on other people's
data & call it research.

It is, the poet thinks, better to travel than arrive — hope
doesn't come into it.

What the poet sees in the rear view is their oeuvre receding

into a light that burns the eyes.

Vertigo

What are you doing in my graveyard?
My heart is a catafalque, my body a crow.
All along it was you — a silverfish in the bouquet.
Anxiety is a bellboy ringing the lobbybell.
Where is the service here? Are there any rooms?
Every time we talk we talk about a room,
a room where we meet, that we might book,
can put our coats in, the coats we care for,
and leave them spread out like vellum
cut from rakish cattle. All along it was you.
I knew it & couldn't know enough to say.
Let's remote the coffin in the hidden river.
Fish with me? News of our death together
has been grossly exaggerated. Print never lies.
Our names? Let's pose for a group photo
with only the two of us. News of my pulse
has been gravely misappropriated. CC me in
with nobody else. Blind copy your swan neck.
Views of my face have been silently copyrighted.

Pass me my crowsuit, I'm going out for a craw
for a while. You think you won't but you'll
write my will. What are you doing in my boneyard?
The barrowboy is hauling in goldfinch.
Sing for me? All the whales are on my windowsill.
Hang my swan in your croak room? Armani
fits well in an upright coffin. Every time we talk
about a room I hear the cattle print their vellum.
Where is the service here? I downloaded matins
an hour ago. It was you all along; you looked
at the spines in my bedroom. Can you hear them?
The underground river has my clavicle in it.
Fish with me? I think you will when the sun runs low
on the obelisk. Swim with me? You will when the tide
gives out. Hawthorns take so long to grow
and I crave mayflower so much in the leap year.
My head is in the catafalque. Those silver boxes
keep me up all night because I know what's in them.
Did you ever see my heart & the open box at once?
Pledge for me then. This suit is a puppet show, my shadow
a crow, my body a barrowboy peeling his marrow.
Sign with me? It's hard to concentrate, being mostly
liquid. Go halves on a bundle then? My upgrade comes

going horizontal. Download a skyhook with me?
You have the hook & I'll take the barb.
Keep lookout for me? Watch me think?
At night the crow lives eating its stomach.

Library

Silence in the library is measured.

The library relies on recirculation for close reading to take place.

Noise in the library is the equivalent to a streaker at a funeral.

The librarian approaching middle age is required to wet his shoes in salt water.

The clearest idea of a successful library is one that moves its books to new spaces to be seen for the first time.

An enquiry is a kind of invisible bridge between where the enquirer is and where they believe they need to be. Good librarians ferry them by boat.

Now that data streams from us like duct tape in a

documented wind, the library has become society's major paradox.

The library is a compass dial on the glass of the ancient city.

It is the library's duty to make each visitor feels as if they've entered a familiar dream.

The library's system is to arrange its books like iron filings around a magnet.

Those who have known real failure are most at home in the library.

The library contains many boxes. If all boxes are opened at once, the library shows its purpose.

Fernando Pessoa aspired to be an archivist in a library & was rejected. His heteronyms appear as one shadow in our minds : a lone drinker in a dark tavern.

The only solace for homesickness is a library : thumbed books are closer to the sheets of your bed than a strange place to sleep.

A poor circulation system can lead to the opposite of a bank run : if all customers bring their books back at once there's not enough space to house them.

Every library's lights are controlled by a hidden circuit board that is only known to the librarian.

The library's success is based on the source of its nearest underground river.

The library without holes is a warehouse.

The library is aware that search engines are not made from possibility but hierarchy. There's no such thing as free internet.

White noise in the library is the only measure of sound amongst its patrons.

The library's future is data and paper. Data. Paper. Data. Paper. Nada. Pater.

Cure

Tincture of lead
Extracts of arsenic
Fox respiratory tracts
Boar's fangs
Scraped ivory
Secretion of beavers
Compacted coral
Ipecacuanha
The cassia tree
Paste of crab's eyes
Goat faeces
Frogs (whole)
Claws of crows
Dog fennel
Weight of lead plates
Human hands
Surgical excision
Bleeding & purging
Radio- and chemo-therapy
Holy waters

August

No one told me parenting was all hardhat & no shoes.
At six years old he carries a notebook for most things.
In 1957, he reads, Laika was a dog that went to space.
I can't tell him — in this sun — that Laika never came back.
He takes notes as I drill the geranium's drainage :
the water stinks, he says.

Anarchitecture

New York artist Gordon Matta-Clark died of pancreatic cancer in 1978, aged 35. His twin brother had committed suicide two years before. Mirrored cells duplicate. The survival rate is 5%. Matta-Clark made holes in buildings, a practice of cutting through piers to see light, digging a gallery basement that was documented, then filled in. Gaps, voids & left-over spaces. Anarchitecture.

Mirrored cells duplicate. Less than 5% survival rate. The most severe pancreatic cancer is Adenocarcinoma. It is also the most common. It starts in the digestive enzymes & is mostly diagnosed when it's broke out from the pancreas. It spread as Matta-Clark worked on the cuttings he called 'probes' : *I just like to get in there and alter it.*

Adenocarcinoma. Anarchitecture.

Voids, gaps & left-over spaces.

Straw

John Whittaker Straw, Labour politician, would not pardon
the Pendle witches, not in 1998, or any time after.
John Whittaker Straw, one of the Blair witches,
who changed his name to that of Wat Tyler's sidekick,
or pseudonymous fiction : Jack Straw.
A name like Black Kat or John Bull, a crack in folklore.
John Whittaker Straw may have stood with Gordon Brown
as John Rakestraw, or Rackstraw, as Jack was known,
and address the house to say 'duplicitous' to weapons
of mass destruction. He did not do that under the name
of the Jack he aped, who was a preacher, or a priest, inciting
a crowd to rise like revenants from an Essex churchyard.
John Whittaker who changed his name to one who confessed
his plans to kill 'all landowners, bishops, monks, canons & rectors
of churches' : his plans to burn down London.
Had Jack watched his daughter violated by a tax collector
and in his anger seethe to see metropolis burned black?
He Jakke Strawe & his meinee, Chaucer wrote,
wooden any Fleminge kill. From Jack's Straw Castle,

a hay wagon on Hampstead Heath, the rebel preached.
John Whittaker Straw took that Jack then served like milk
for thirteen years the Labour cabinet.

Body

On Valentine's the bones of Henry V reconstructed in
  leather.

Your birthday : the wax casket of Elizabeth at Charing X.

On All Hallows : the cropped skull of Cromwell kicked
  along Whitehall.

September 3rd : Pepys dared not wear his periwig for fear
  of infection.

Katherine de Valois in Westminster Abbey : the body lifted
  from its coffin & kissed.

January 13th : the finger of Thomas à Becket cast inside an
  oval reliquary.

The dead walk through lavender by laudanum.

With each death a desire for body. For witness. For song.

Cemetery

Obelisk my SMS.
Graves turn to silk when light fails.
Text me. Text my face.
X marks none to three score years.
Words washed. Touch.
Lie down in this bath of topaz.
Two paths : rats or dissenters.
Riotous the grass (lie with us?).
Graves are doorsteps to. Obelisk.
Text this obelisk. Rats.
Dissenters three score
years when light fails.
X marks grass. Riotous
to touch. Text fails.
Topaz washed in light. Years.
Turn to me. Lie with us?
Graves are words. Graves of us.
Riotous dissenters in this grass
of topaz. Text this. X my SMS.

Two words : light and fails.

Years are obelisks. Two words.

Two : touch and face. Touch.

Touch where words washed.

Touch text. Cut and place.

Cut and Couldn't.

Graves are lies, are light.

Turn to silk when words fail.

Lie. Lie with us.

O my love we came for this. *This.*

No Word

for the parents who lost children at the Manchester Arena bombing

For the death of a child there is none. No word.
A space where there was one. A pillow. Wind.
People say lack of sleeplessness is amnesia.
It is anger. Memories attached to cloth. Lack.
A last look on a. Missing face. Milk. Walking.
There is no word for the death of your child.

Bowie

'David Bowie died of liver cancer after a period of ill-health'
NME.COM

ZIGGY STARDUST had just one liver,
ALADDIN SANE, the aspen white of the YOUNG AMERICAN
had just one liver,
THIN WHITE DUKE, THE GOBLIN KING, just one liver,
MAJOR TOM, the Anonymous Mime Star,
just one liver across THREE MUSKETEERS
— the deck of cards is on the floor —
the phase of the EGYPTIAN GOD had just one liver,
one liver for THE MAN WHO FELL TO EARTH,
in the PUPPET PHASE he was the one with the liver,
there was just one liver
in the period of the VAMPIRE, a toothless skull
sourced from just one liver

DAVID ROBERT JONES
one life

Pink

'Come on you raver, you seer of visions, come on you painter, you
piper, you prisoner, and shine!'
PINK FLOYD

Can I go now, you said, sat on my bedroom floor,
after I'd made you listen to 'Shine on You Crazy Diamond
(parts 1-5)'. I said that was just the first half.
I showed you the sleeve of the two men shaking hands,
    one of them on fire
against the backdrop of a pharmaceutical white city,
or perhaps that was just how you felt
after the evening's half quart of discount vodka.
Your body would not yield to spirits in your lifetime,
not before cancer had worked its process
called the chemical handshake —
the cancer dresses in the same suit as the healthy cells
and tricks them into shaking hands while eating the tissue.
The man on the sleeve who's not in flame
feels the banked log of heat spread along his arm,
trap inside the lining of his suit; black smoke

Houdinis his face, pushing him down in a heap
of captured flame. The man on fire is consumed by it too :
having achieved what he set out to do.

Stockings

'My good sweete mouse ... though the sickness be round about you, yett by his mercy itt may escape your house ... And, Jug, I pray you, lett my orayng tawny stokins of wolen be dyed a very good blak against I com hom, to wear in the winter'

EDWARD ALLEYN, LETTER TO HIS WIFE, 1ST AUGUST 1593

In plague-time, dye my orange stockings black,
keep check on my rents & garden of spinach,
good heart & loving mouse,
leave water at your door ere you sleep
and in your windows keep a store of rue
and herb of grace against the darkness,
there is no news other than my health
and that today we are in marriage
for a complete six months,
if I was not of the Lord's Strange Men
here in Chelmsford
I would forthwith return to the Bankside Clink
to dance with dyed stockings at our hearth
(dye them a good deep black for the winter months)
while the black spoor of the Plague, my mouse,
is pressed to the door, for to button our kiss.

Coupling

These accidents of body & place called marriage.
Or is it the destiny of genes that splits the union
of two rings by one box into startled vernacular?
My father a *victim*, my mother a *survivor*.

Anchor

'The root of tongues ends in a spentout cancer'
DYLAN THOMAS

The inward craft enters hollow cells, dissolves them down,
breaks on sea's fixed shores & flags new forms.
The craft ploughs wormholes. Light leaves spoors.
The cells that died at growth blast new life.
Winter freaked by blighting spring. The inward craft
blinds oncologists, knits stats to the stone of fact.

Anchor clones anchor. Seabeds explode Hiroshima's dust.
John Dorys blossom. Lovelocks unclose a past of touch.
The inward craft roaches its way beneath your Thames.
Walls break in forgotten docks. Ships dissolve on fragile
    shores.

Ditch

I will see you at the cowslips of Black Ditch.
I'll have a burned heart & a thread of Milton's hair,
Blake's hawthorn & a cup of blood.
Meet me at Black Ditch; we'll flyerbomb the estate,
where the road cuts the Rye & stops
in a cloud of fieldfares & foraging choughs.
Will we meet on Catacombs Path or Dissenters Road?
Washed on the stone or dead on the steps?
Flick light, light flicker : until I come back.

ACKNOWLEDGEMENTS

Poems in this book have appeared in the following magazines: *Disclaimer Magazine, Manhattan Review, Poetry London, The Wolf.* My thanks to all editors involved.

'&' was written for the anthology *Asterism: an anthology of poems inspired by punctuation* (laudanum, 2016), edited by Tiffany Anne Tondut.

'Alice' was commissioned for *Alice: Ekphrasis at the British Library* (Joy Lane Publishing, 2016), edited by Emer Gillespie, Abegail Morley and Catherine Smith.

'Cemetery' was published as a postcard by Penned in the Margins and released with the limited edition of *Cenotaph South: Mapping the Lost Poets of Nunhead Cemetery*, published in 2016.

'Light' was commissioned by James Wilkes for the Wellcome Collection and UCL event *On Light* in May 2015 and published in *Refracted Light: 20 Poets Respond to Jackson Mac Low's Light Poems* (Renscombe Press, 2015).

'Voice' was written for *Poems for Roddy*, a pamphlet of poems for Roddy Lumsden edited by Lavinia Singer (2017).

'Library' was commissioned by Rick Myers and published in his limited edition artist's book *Faraday's Synaptic Gap: Coda to the Exhibition* (Arc Editions, 2016).

'Love' was commissioned by the Laurence Sterne Trust for the exhibition *Paint Her to Your Own Mind* in 2016. Thanks to Patrick Wildgust.

'Vertigo' was commissioned by Simon Barraclough in response to Hitchcock's *Vertigo* and was performed as part of *Vertiginous* at the BFI, London on Friday 13th July 2018.

'Straw' was published in *Atlantic Drift: An Anthology of Poetry and Poetics* (Arc Publications & Edge Hill University Press, 2017), edited by James Byrne and Robert Sheppard.

The phrase 'the inward craft' in 'Anchor' is from Lucretius' *On the Nature of the Universe*. There is an echo of Dylan Thomas's rhythm and imagery in this poem and of T.S. Eliot in the opening of the poem 'Cancer'.

Thanks to James Byrne for a close reading and comments on these poems.

A massive thanks to Sarah Crewe for reading these poems in manuscript form and making crucial suggestions which have improved this collection.